If You're Reading This,
I Love You

Jair Griffin

BookLeaf Publishing

India | USA | UK

Presentation by *BookLeaf Publishing*

Web: www.bookleafpub.com

E-mail: info@bookleafpub.com

ISBN: 9789367399521

First edition 2024

I dedicate this book to everybody on a journey off the beaten path. To the trailblazers who are finding their own way, and being a light in the darkness.

This is for all the leaders and followers of every discipline showcasing how to discover the light from within.

For everyone looking for a way out, and all of those finding things out on their own.

All the explorers and voyagers paving their own way, and everyone aiming for a target that nobody else seems to see.

I see you, and I support you.

Don't let anyone else stop you from finishing what you started.

ACKNOWLEDGEMENT

Thank you, dear reader, for your time and your open-mindedness. If you're reading this, it means that you're ready to start thinking about life in a brand new way, and I'm proud of you. It might be a lot to digest, so take your time and let it marinate. If you don't agree with everything that's said, it's okay. It took me a while to accept many of the concepts in here, and even longer to embrace them. Now it's time for me to release them. And it's up to you to receive them.

PREFACE

I'm no different from you. I'm just a person with some dreams and a few callings I've tried to run from. Writing this book falls into both of these categories.

As an artist, I love seeing what other people create, yet I've been gatekeeping my own creations long enough. I went to school to study music and philosophy, yet I still find myself lacking credibility. I am qualified by the same thing that qualifies everyone else to do what they do, which is purely the desire itself. Don't let lack of experience disqualify you from chasing your own dreams. They were given to you for a reason because you're the one who's supposed to bring them into fruition.

Just like you, I must face my own fears and fight my own battles. This book is the result of both of those.

I'm here to show you that if I can do what I've been called to do, then you'll be able to do what you came here to do. Nobody else can do it for you.

Thanks for Being Here

If you're reading this,
Congratulations!
You made it to today,
Despite all your trials and tribulations.
And it looks like you're here to stay.

You made it this far and lived through everything you've
been through.
You're the only one in existence that did everything you
did.
Other people may say they could've done it,
Or that they could've done it better.
But you actually did it,
And you made it look easy.

How demure, how mindful,
How elegant and graceful.
It's giving Main Character energy
The way you move through life so effortlessly.

But deep beneath the surface,
I know it was hard.
You couldn't have gotten this far
Without exceeding some limits.
And you've probably wanted to quit
More than you care to admit.

So thank God you didn't.
I'm glad you're still here.
The whole world is made better
Because we still have you in it.

You're the only person in existence that could ever be you.
That's why you put yourself here.
We desperately needed you.
So continue to be yourself.
There's nothing better to do.
Nobody could ever do it any better than you.

You've gone through so many ups and downs,
And held on while life spun you around.
You made it through thick and thin
At times when nobody helped you out.
You even stood up for others
When you didn't feel cared about.

You loved when you needed it.
You gave until you were drained.
You took care of others even though you were pained,
All in the hopes that it would make its way back to you.
I assure you that none of your efforts were in vain.

You are seen and you are loved.
Countless blessings are on their way.
I promise that life gets better,
It was designed that way.
The storms are passing over.
Your peace will be here to stay.

So celebrate yourself
Just for making it to today.
If you weren't here with us,
Things just wouldn't be the same.

Thank you for being here,
Thank you for being you,
And thank you so much
For who you are and all you do.

If Only You Knew

I've got devastating news.
Ignorance isn't bliss.
Butterflies can't see their own wings,
Did you know this?

As beautiful as they are,
They're cursed to never notice
They can't see what we see
And I think it's bogus

Do you think it was set up to be this way on purpose?
With their mesmerizing blessing lying just outside their
consciousness,
Forever evading their limited awareness?

As pretty as they may be,
Butterflies will never see
The beauty and wonder that live within their wings

How tragic it is
That they'll never be able to recognize
How stunning they are
Or how intricately they were designed.
It's truly a travesty
Because their beauty is divine.

Each one is doomed to be blind
To the magic they leave behind
And all the joy that they bring
With the movements of their wings.

They have no clue of what becomes
of their tiny little flutters
or how they positively impact all of their surroundings.
They fly around their gardens,
Admiring all the beauty they see in others,
Unaware that they're equally majestic and captivating.

How immaculate they are is beyond them,
Yet all they can do is flaunt what they've been given.
All they can be is their beautiful selves
And present themselves as the gifts they are
To all those that surround them.

A butterfly never gets to experience
How valuable it is from its perspective.
Pictures don't do them any justice.
Being in their presence is a miracle to witness.

You are just like every butterfly you've seen.
Cursed with the burden of the ignorance of your beauty,
Living your life oblivious to what happens when you're
seen,
Thinking you weren't simply the epitome of beauty.

Let's take a few moments to appreciate your beingness.
Let's take a bit of time to acknowledge your
accomplishments.
Let's pause to look in the mirror and reflect
On all the beauty and wonder that's been bestowed within
you.

You went through a metamorphosis
And you're now effectively changing others.
Your very existence ripples out and reaches more than
you've imagined.
You're doing way more than you can begin to comprehend.

Even though you may not see it,
Trust that you're here on purpose.
God made you,
And everything about you,
As intricately as the beauty
That lives in a butterfly's wings.

The World is Our Canvas

We brush ourselves across the surface of this earth,
Painting it with all of the beauty that we are.
We dance around this planet with the colors of our auras,
Mixing and mingling them with every interaction.

We create a beautiful mosaic of experiences and
expressions
By simply being who we are and flowing without
suppression.
We become a vibrant tapestry of living, breathing art
By all of us coming together and playing a unique part.

We are a sacred symphony, conducted by life itself.
The spirit of creation flows through us all.
It's the rhythm that moves everything in eternity.
And the power that we use to create anything at all.
But with creative liberty comes responsibility.

In this life, we create what we'd like to see.
We do this by deciding who we'll be.
You can be, do, and have anything you can imagine.
It's your birthright to experience opulence and abundance.

All of existence is always in full support of you.
God, the Universe, Everything, and All That Exists is on
your side.
Call it what you like,
It's not complete without you in it.

Every note is important no matter how redundant.
Every shade is an indispensable participant.
Every beaming ray of sunshine is equally radiant.
Every drop of water in the ocean is equally significant.

There might be some times when we all feel invisible,
Or that the world might be better off without us.
I guarantee you, that couldn't be further from the truth.
No matter what you feel, you'll never be replaceable.

We Need You

Life is a puzzle and it's not complete without each piece.
No matter how insignificant you may feel,
You're just as important as any other.
If you weren't here, the world would be missing out.

Every creation within creation is one with all of creation.
All of creation wouldn't All
If we were missing any single one of these creations.
The world would not be whole without each one of its
parts.
The sum is the greatest when each piece is in the right spot.

There might be a void you could be filling
If you stopped avoiding your purpose.
You would fit where you belong if you were living as you
were designed.
We were called to do greater works, that's how we get
aligned
We were meant to be our fullest selves in the image of
creation.

It's okay to take up space, especially where you belong.
You belong right where you are
Remember who put you here,
Remember why you're alive,
And then remember why you're still alive.

God designed you to be yourself while you're here.
You're a part of something bigger than you.
It's grander than your vision.
But it can't happen without you.
So walk by faith and not just sight.

Believe that everything will be alright.
Trust that you'll end up in the places and spaces that fit you
just right.

And the best part is, you're already in the right spot.
Because the only place to be is right here, right now.
You are the centerpiece of the puzzle of your life.

What's Holding You Back?

What is a musician that doesn't make music?
What is an artist that doesn't make art?
Who is a singer that doesn't sing?
What is a creator that doesn't create?

Why are so many people not doing the things that bring
them the most
life, joy, and fulfillment?
So many people are lost, scared, confused, stuck,
And otherwise not being or doing what makes them happy.
Including myself at times.

Why?

What are we afraid of?

If we're afraid of our own power, why even is that?
Why do we care ultimately about our own judgment than
the judgments of others
Whether close to us or far away?

What makes us so immobilized by fear
That we don't share what we're capable of with the world?

What are these energetic blocks and where do they come
from?
Most importantly, how do we overcome them?

It makes no sense for us to hold ourselves back,
Unless we feel like we're protecting ourselves from
something,
Or someone.
Why else would we put ourselves on a leash?

What happens if we release our shackles and become our
full selves?

What's the worst that could happen?

And on the other hand,
What's the best thing that could happen?

What if you could change the whole world and inspire
millions
By doing the thing that you already accepted as a part of
who you are?

Even when we release our parents' expectations of
ourselves,
There will always be other people in our lives
That we won't want to disturb
By being our fullest selves,
So we hide and play small.

But ultimately,
We're only hiding from ourselves
Since we're the ones that decide
whose judgment matters in our lives
and who to hide ourselves from.

Of course, it's all for good reason.
But at some point,
We must come out of hiding or we'll die before we live.

That is the reality of the situation.

Imagine if your favorite artist hid their whole life
And never released your favorite song,
Or the song that you listen to when you're sad
That helps you get through hard times.

What if all the designers of your favorite outfit
Were too scared to be themselves?
What if the architects involved in your favorite place
Never designed it or built it?
What if the most innovative contributors didn't contribute?
The world wouldn't be what it is right now.

And what if everyone decided to do all the things they
could do?
What if you decided to be great, take up space, and make
an impact?
Imagine how much greater your own life would be
If you released all the burdens and shackles
Keeping you from creating the way you were created to
create.

Now imagine if everyone did the things
That were placed in their hearts to be and do.

Think about all the unreleased songs, books, movies,
podcasts,
Inventions, designs, ways of being and doing, ideas,
projects,
and all the other contributions to the life we all share
that people take to their graves.

Do you want to live out your dreams or die with them?

You have these dreams, goals, and aspirations for a reason.
These gifts are not for you to keep, but to share.

It is a disservice to God, the universe, and yourself
To continue playing small and keeping your gifts hidden
from even yourself.

Imagine how great you could be if you believed in yourself
Enough to take action on your visions and artistic desires.

Imagine how much happier everyone would be
If we all lived out our dreams and encouraged each other to
do so.

Imagine if we were all encouraged and empowered to be
ourselves,
And pursue our passions no matter how trivial
Or outlandish they might seem
To those that don't see the visions that we were given.

No matter how small your dreams are,
they could positively impact countless lives.
And we'll never know how many, or to what degree,
Until we pursue them and see for ourselves.
We'll never know how great or powerful we're capable of
being
Until we find out by living it out firsthand.

I empower you to follow your dreams, passions, goals,
wishes, and desires,
and see where they take you.

Learn all you can about your passions.
Discover all there is to find about them
and enjoy the ride you end up in.

Find ways to be yourself and let yourself be seen
If that's what it takes.
Take steps to come out of hiding and to accept yourself
So that you can be accepted wherever it is you truly belong.
You might even be accepted where you are once you accept
yourself fully.

It's not always easy coming to terms with how powerful
you are,
Especially with the responsibility that great power brings.
Even if you don't step into your power,
The responsibility is still there.
And it's easier to handle if you step into your power before
it's too late.

If there is a hole that you can fill,
You must fill it.
Or someone else may or may not come along
And fill it with or without you.
If you want that hole filled,
And only you can fill it,
Then it is your responsibility,
And you must use your great power,
Or both you and the hole will live unfulfilled
Until you die.

Fill up your holes
Take up your spaces
And you will live happily and die fulfilled.

You die whichever way you choose to live.

It's much better to live a life of contentment
If you wish to be content at the end of it all.
It's easier to do the things you want to do
Instead of only watching other people do what you were
meant to do
If you wish to be fulfilled throughout life and into death.
It's more efficient and practical to take and create
opportunities to be great
When you can
Instead of wishing and waiting until you can't.

Carpe diem.
Carpe noctem.

Sieze whatever time you can get ahold of
And live your live before it's too late.

Memento vivere.
Memento mori.

Death is the only guarantee in life.
And if you want it to be pleasant,
Do all you can to live your live as fully as you can
While you're still here.

Even if you believe in reincarnation,
You only get to live this particular life one time
Before whatever happens in whichever afterlife.
We all procrastinate enough within one lifetime.
There's no need to put off living until after death.

Do it here.
Do it now.

Be yourself in this present moment
While it's here.
Because, no matter what,
It won't be here again.

We're All Gonna Die, So We Might As Well Vibe

Life is a means to an end.
Death is that end.
Death is also a means to an end.
And that ending is a new beginning.

A new life, a rebirth,
A neverending story,
Told for perpetuity,
It never gets old.

Life and death are complementary.
They feed into each other,
providing the other its meaning.

Leaves and flowers grow and bloom
Then they fall to the earth at the end of their season.
Their beauty has a reason,
They become nutrients for the trees.
Just like when pine cones fall and decay into the soil
To continue the story acting as seeds.

Life and death are a cyclical process.
They are pointless without each other.
In the same way, those things that look like failures
Are steps on your path to success.

Everything that dies contributes to the next thing to be alive
Every update owes its life equally
To the shortcomings and successes
Of all of its predecessors.

Everything you've ever done,
That bloomed or withered,
For a short time or long,
Has been contributing to you and your growth all along.
It's all been conspiring together to make something special;
Life as we know it, featuring you with your song!

Your melody is a necessity in the universe,
Your vibration belongs in the mix of existence
Your frequency holds divine significance
And your track is the life of the party.

But ultimately, like all good things,
the dance must come to an end.
The lights come on,
and we all go back home.

Yes, it will all be over at some point.
And then a new thing will begin.
And that will die, too,
Giving life to the next thing.

Every life and death feed back into the life of all that is
Then all that is will expand until it inevitably collapses.
It will grow and decay,
Inhale and exhale,
Until it breathes its very last breath.

Nothing lasts forever.
That's what gives everything its meaning.
It's your job to choose what anything means to you.

Life is inherently meaningless,
Sometimes even senseless,
The only thing that matters is what all of this means to you.

Know Thyself

Who are you?
No, who are you really?

Not your interests, not your name, not your belief system.
Not the car you drive or how you move about the world.
Not the memories you've accumulated or the intellect
you've acquired.

Who are you?
More importantly,
What are you?

Are you your mind?
Are you your body?
Are you your spirit?

Not quite.
For all of these things are yours,
They're in your possession.
You cannot be a thing that you possess.

If you are the one that possesses these things,
Along with all of their traits and qualities,
Then what on earth would that leave you to be?

Ownership makes you the owner.
Stewardship makes you the steward.
Your body is a vessel,
Making you the captain of the ship.

If you're the one in charge of your body,
Then you are not your body.

If you are the one aware of yourself,
Then you cannot be yourself,
As it is, by definition, "your" self.

If you are not your mind, your body, or your spirit,
For all of these merely pertain to you
Then what could that possibly make you?

You are life itself,
Experiencing itself
From your unique and invaluable perspective.
You are the one watching your mind, body, and spirit
As they learn to get along within your self.

You are the one observing your life through your eyes.
You are the one witnessing your life's experiences.
You are the consciousness that perceives your life
And processes it within your awareness.

You're the owner, the director, and the manager,
Yet you're still aware of these processes.
You're the one who's conscious of your awareness.
You're able to observe yourself in the act of perceiving.

You might feel like the driver,
But you're actually the passenger.
You're the viewer,
The one that's watching it all happen live.

You are the one getting carried by your body.
You feel what it senses in all your experiences.
You hear what your mind receives from the ethers.
You listen to your brain and how it's been programmed to
think.

You are connected to,
Yet still separate from,
All of these functions.
They even operate better
Without your interference.

Life starts when you get out of the way.
So sit back, relax, and enjoy the ride
While you let life unfold before your very eyes.

You Are One With Life Itself

If you ask, "Hello? Is anybody in there?"
Any response is a yes.
Even a "no" is still a yes.
Because somebody has to be in there
To say anything at all.

In the same way,
If anything is moving,
It's always because something living moved it.
Whether it be a physical hand or an invisible hand,
Something living set it into motion.

The whole universe is moving
Along with everything in it,
Therefore everything in it must be alive.
Set into motion by the same living thing.

We have this concept of inanimate objects,
but inanimate simply means not breathing on its own.
Not moving according to its own free will.
It is living on borrowed life
From whatever creator took their life
And set the smaller one into a path of motion.

Even us, animated objects,
Are breathing borrowed air.
Our bodies are inanimate,
Yet we still breathe with them.

The breaths in our lungs are not ours to keep.
The life flowing through us is passing through
momentarily.
Our whole lifetimes are on borrowed time.

All the magic within us appears to be our own,
But no one owns any of it.
We're under sacred contracts.
Our bodies are out on a lease.

Simply because we have the illusion
Of moving ourselves about,
And experiencing free will,
Doesn't mean that our lives our truly our own.

We are all parts of one living breathing organism
that we call God, the universe, source, life itself, or all that
exists.
It's all the same thing.
In fact, it's the only thing.
It's existence itself.

If a house is made of brick,
You'd call it a brick house house.
In the exact same way, we are all one with God.
We are all made of the one divine substance
It's the only material.
That's why we call it Source.

We use it to create and recreate everything else,
But it all starts off in its image and likeness.
What we do with our lives is up to us to choose,
But it is all a part of the same one life.

Life is a game,
And it's a game of tag.
We're running from the truth,
But it's everywhere.
Eventually, we'll all get tired of playing these games,
littered with violence and the illusion of separation.

And that's when all the real fun begins,
When we live lives filled with love and connection.

T.A.G. You're It!
We're all It.
Thou Art God.
Embrace It.
The Generator, Operator, and Destroyer
Of all that which is.
Like it or love it, you are It.

It is the life in the air that we breathe.
It doesn't belong to us.
It merely flows through us.
And we get to enjoy It as It happens
So live life knowing that you're one with It.

The Way of Nature

The trees don't live in perpetual fear of a jealous God
Smiting them down for being a sinner.

The ocean isn't scared that some higher power
Is micromanaging it and criticizing its every move.

The butterflies don't cover their beauty in shame,
Rather, they flaunt it with elegance and grace,
By simply being their beautiful selves.

The wolves don't try to convert other packs
To howling at the moon according to their particular rules.

Hyenas don't fight each other over money.

The grass doesn't compare itself to the grass on the other
side.
It just grows without competing.

The clouds don't try to fit each other into molds
Of how the ideal cloud should behave.

Nature doesn't argue about semantics

It simply is and it simply does.
It does not spend time caring or worrying
about the thoughts in the mind of another
As if they were their own.

It still acts in accordance to the cycles in life,
But it does not acknowledge any need
To force facts or belief systems onto any other.

So why do we?
Why do we care so much?

More so,
Why do we go about acting on this care
In the ways that we do?

Why do we stress so much about the well-being of another
So much so that we act harshly towards the individuals
That we supposedly care so much about?

Why do we love so intensely that it manifests hatefully?
Why do we hurt in our attempts to help?
Why does saving so often turn into smothering?
Especially when we aren't fully certain
About what exactly it is we're saving anyone from.

Ask anyone for a concrete answer
About all the specific details of why they're right
And everyone else is wrong.

Ask them to explain what they're afraid of from start to
finish,
Ask them how it happens as well as how they know.

Also, ask them if they know,
Or if they only believe in the words they were told
Without question.

See if they're sure.
And ask them why they're so certain.

The real issues begin when we care about
The ideologies in other peoples' minds
When we don't fully adhere to our own.
Condemning another for something

And doing the same thing when no one else can see you
Is far from productive.
Preaching without practicing is beneficial to no one at all.

If we all learned how to love ourselves first
unconditionally.
I guarantee that it would make loving thy neighbor
significantly easier.
Imagine if we saw ourselves with loving eyes instead of
judgmental ones.
How can we love anyone else if we don't know how to love
ourselves?

What if we tended to the problems in our own homes
Instead of prioritizing everything else in life?
What if we dealt with our own emotions
Instead of letting them run wild
With the looming risk of them coming out to hurt
someone?

What if we prioritized peace?
What if we solved all the problems that are ours
And only our own to solve?
Do we care enough about each other to love ourselves?
Would it be more productive
To fill the world with love one's self at a time?

If we like where we are with the current state of affairs,
Then there is no need to change anything.
However, if we are anything less than completely, 100%
satisfied,
Then we have some adjustments to make.
Only a few.

All we have to do is what works
And stop doing what doesn't.

All we really need to do this is radical honesty
About what does work and what doesn't.
And if it doesn't work,
Then we must be willing to release it
And make space for what might
As we work to figure out what will.

This means having a willingness to try.
To try new things, old things,
The same things differently,
And different things the same way
That the familiar ones were used.

This is all still under the condition that we are indeed
Any bit displeased with how we've been doing things
As a family of humans inhabiting this planet we call Earth.
If everything's fine, then we have nothing to do.

The truth is everything really is fine
And there really is nothing we can do.
Nothing at all.
For everything is exactly as it should be.
Life is perfect as it is,
Moving in the direction it chooses,
as it prefers,
when it prefers to,
and precisely as it intends to.

If you, the individual, would like to see a change,
You must make it within yourself.
The individual is only capable of changing their own self,
And has no power over the collective.
Any attempts to change the collective against its will will
be fruitless.
Growth is a matter of the individual.
Fortunately, the ocean is made up of individual drops

That can all choose to individually
Grow, change, and evolve at their own rate.
And by being connected to the fullness of the ocean,
Impact the whole thing by changing itself for its own sake.

It is not the business of the drop to shift the tides.
It is the only business of the part to its role,
And by doing so, it improves the whole.
Now, if you still want to change the world,
change yourself.

If you still want anything for anyone else,
Give it to yourself and let them find it in you
Whenever they decide they're ready for it
And if they never are,
At least you have it.

Your life is about who?
And you're concerned about what?

Why?

It's your life,
So if you're going to care about anything prioritize you.
Focus on being the change you'd like to see in the world
And be happy if you see your change reflecting back to you
in other drops.

Be the light in the darkness.
Be that which you seek,
Or you risk never finding it anywhere else.
The only way to know what you'll find when you're
looking for
Is to embody it and bring it into existence for yourself
Then be surprised when the mirror of life reflects you back
to yourself.

We Are Connected

Every leaf on a tree is equally a part of the tree
As a branch or the trunk, or the roots underneath.
Every drop of water is equally a part of the ocean the same
way
That everything in existence is one with the divine
substance.

There is nothing else.

All that is
Is one with all that is.
You are one with it.

We are all one with it.
We are all collectively the great I AM.
We are the great WE ARE.

Down from the smallest quark of the smallest electron in
the smallest atom
Up to the biggest star in the biggest galaxy
In the biggest universe in the multiverse.

We, together and collectively, comprise that which is.
We are the deciders of fate
And the voices of destiny.
We are the bees that make up the hive,
The ants that make up the colony,
And the planets that make up the solar system.

We are neurons in the brain of God
And thoughts in the universal mind.
We are formed out of the one divine substance,

Created in its image and likeness,
For we are it.

The power of eternity is flowing through our veins.
Magic is riddled throughout our DNA.
You are flowing through everyone else as they are all
flowing through you.
For there is no one else.
We are all you.
And you are all me.
We are all the same self pretending to be different.

We are all the same actor,
Assuming different roles, identities, and archetypes
All just to live out the drama of being human,
Or a stapler, a book, or a worm,
A speck of dust, a cathedral, or an instrument,
A bad idea, a grain of rice, or whatever chooses to come to
physicality
To be experienced by itself
From various perspectives for a temporary time.

Deep down, we all know this.

We all know that we never left heaven
Despite all the hell we've created through our questionable
decisions
As a species occupying this planet.

We all know that we're God pretending to be man,
Life pretending to be death,
And love pretending to be hate.
Our souls know all of this,
But we have all been collectively feigning ignorance
And pretending that we don't know the eternal truths of
life.

We have let this show go on long enough in its current
condition.
It's time to turn the lights back on and remember who we
are.

We are all God.
We are all it.
We are all each other pretending not to be.
We are souls pretending to be humans.
And it's time to start acting like our true selves now.

It's okay.
We've had our fun living in the illusions of separation,
But I guarantee you,
Living in remembrance is much more peaceful.
Choosing to honor the divinity within all things
And cherishing the divine spark within each of us
Would stop the need for war overnight.

We'd get along as a human family
In this home that we call Earth.
We'd choose de-escalation over violence every time.
We'd share with equality and equity in every aspect of our
lives.
We might even mess around and respect each other's
religions
And begin to celebrate our cultural differences.

Maybe I'm being delusional.
Maybe that's exactly what it takes
To dispel the illusions that we've been living in.

Maybe we should all disillusion ourselves
From these ways of existing that are no longer conducive
To the things that we say we want for ourselves.

Maybe we should consider remembering who we really are
And what we really intend to do with our lives on this
planet.

Maybe.
Just maybe.
It might even be fun.

Finding Resolution

I'm not atheist or agnostic.
You could say I'm diagnostic.
I came here to shed light on some issues that we can fix.
I can already tell you now, the answers are hidden within.
That's probably why we're still looking for directions.

Living life as we've been doing is less than sustainable
Faith alone won't get us to where we say we want to go.
We must change our course of action if we wish to actually
end up
Being, doing, and having what is is truly preferable.

Are we waiting for Jesus to come and take the wheel?
We must steer ourselves and navigate through these realms
and planes.
How else will we get there?
Not by staying the same.

How long will we stay where we are,
Stuck in our ways,
Waiting for someone to come down and rescue us
From what we've done to our own living space?
We have all the resources and tools we could need.
We must use them to fix ourselves and troubleshoot our
issues

When will we follow the instructions
That have already been left behind?
When will we come back together
And leave our unproductive habits behind?

If we follow our directions and listen to our intuition,
Then we can operate smoothly and maintain what we've
been given.
We can put the fun in our functions and put our wisdom
into practice.
We can take accountability for all of our actions
And live a life of integrity with harmonious integration.
We can make life better by using our imagination.

Remember, ignorance is a tool
It shows us exactly what we need to know.
It identifies what we need to fix.
And we've already solved all our problems.

But it's up to us now to find resolution.
We must go through the motions to re-solve our problems.
Because we already know all the answers.

We have to use our future perspective to see it.
Look ahead and look inside.
What don't you know?
What don't you do?
You already know what does and doesn't work.
It will…
If you fix it in the future that you choose.

It's already done.
It's all already finished.
Everything transpired exactly as intended.
It turned out better than you ever envisioned

Because the ceiling of the physical mind
Is the floor of the higher mind.
Your higher self is the mastermind
That's guiding you through space and time.

So let yourself move with it.
And go with the flow.
Surrender to what you still have yet to know.

Allow yourself to get informed and move in formation.
Use your discernment to find your element.
It might be in a different environment.

You have to change your mind to know what you meant.
Alternate your mentality to manipulate your reality.
This is the message that's always being sent.

With this,
We have to power to influence our governments.
We constitute them,
We, the people,
That's what they meant.

We have to get in order to form a more perfect union.
Our bonds are broken.
We no longer choose covalence.
Our words are slowly becoming more and more incoherent.
We have to come close and hear each other
To make it all make sense together.

Sometimes you just have to think about things differently,
And they'll resolve themselves inadvertently.
Live your life backwards.
Do it in reverse from the end.

Invert Your Perspective

I've been to the end.
Don't worry, it already happened.
Trust me, it was great.
Everything turned out better than you imagined.

You said it yourself when I spoke to you tomorrow.
You were pleasantly delighted because you relaxed yourself
today.
You did what you had to do to get where you needed to go
In the past as well as in the future that you chose.

You decided right now that you would always trust
yourself.
And that you would align with your highest self every
single day.
You chose to believe that everything would be okay,
And that it's better to feel that way anyway.

The future already holds the best possible outcome.
Congratulate yourself because you already lived it.
Now we let it live through us by walking as if we are it.
Embody the highest version of yourself
By living what you already decided.

Walk backwards on the path that you already took.
Live your life knowing you did what it took.
Go explore, knowing you're guided,
Follow the path that you set for yourself.
See it now because you've already walked it.
It leads to the present moment from the moment you sent it.

Anything you can imagine has already happened.
See yourself living the life of your dreams
Focus on the life that you prefer to choose,
Then do whatever it takes to become that you.

No matter what you do,
It's already you.
You've always been the person you thought you would be.
The you that, deep down, you always knew you could be.

Your dreams have already manifested
You're already out there living them
And you left yourself clues to retrace all your steps
Don't overthink it, it's all in your head.

Trust yourself.
Listen to your guidance.
It's coded,
So you might have to decipher it in silence.

Listen to your advice.
Do what you think is right.
Do what you know is representative of your light.

Our souls are cheering us on from beyond space and time,
Informing ourselves from the future in which we choose.
It's up to you to decide who you listen to
Only you can decide what you're actually going to do.

But just know that you already did it.
It's already been decided.
In each and every moment you choose.

We travel through time, one frame at a time.
Each one branching off into its own string of future
timelines.

Every decision in totality leaves a ripple in infinity,
The ocean that contains every possible reality.
Do what you did in the one you preferred.

The machine has an algorithm.
You manipulate it frequently.
You get what you choose
Not just mentally, but vibrationally.
You get back what you put in it.
Your life is all up to you.

If you listen to yourself,
You'll find consistent synchronicity.
It's a rumble of divine interference.
It's the sound of the waves in the oceans of eternity
Crashing on the sands of time.

You're tuning in to the frequency of God.
So relax into yourself
And turn in, to your creator.

It was you all along.
You did this to yourself.
You did it because,
At some points in time,
You wanted to.

It's Between You and You

Good mourning.
Good grievances.

We're all as good as dead.
The ending of our lives has already occurred.
We haven't gotten there yet,
But the book is already written
With every single one of its possible endings.

Somewhere in the multiverse,
Everything you wanted, you achieved.
Somewhere else, you accomplish a little over nothing.

Here, you've already amounted to something.
But are you on track to accomplishing everything?
Some version of you is somewhere in the multiverse,
Living out your very best life.
You're living your dream life in an alternate reality.

In this life, you have everything you've ever wanted.
You've gone everywhere you wanted to be,
Seen everything you wanted to see,
And did everything you wanted to do.
Somewhere out there in the multiverse
Of infinite possibilities.

Is this the reality where you live your best life?
Is this the one with the best possible outcome?
Is this the universe where you do what it takes?
Do you have the courage to manifest your dreams
In this specific lifetime on this version of Earth?

Are you the you that does what you want to do?

There's a lot of you's out there.
Which one do we have here?
Are you the realest you?
It's entirely up to you.
The only competition is you.

Not only you yesterday,
But every you across the multiverse.
And you're a powerful individual.
Some other versions of you are pushing limits
That you don't even know you have.

You might be outdoing some versions of you,
But there's a lot of yous out there using your current energy
and passions
To do everything you want to do.
Those theoretical versions of you are really out there
Hypothetically doing everything you can think of.

Will you be the realest you in existence?
Can you be the most authentic you that there is?
Are you willing to be your most powerful self?
All you have to do is simply be yourself.
And stop trying to live life as anyone else.

No one else can be you for you
No one else can live your life as you
No one else can even attempt to be you
We specifically need you to be the one to live your life.

So let your mortality motivate you
To be the best possible version of you
The best part is
You're already the best you

Even you couldn't be better than yourself

All those other versions of you that you compare yourself
Didn't have what it takes to actually live your life.
It takes a lot to be you, so give yourself some credit
Don't think that anyone else could ever be you
Not even a hypothetical version of you.

So continue being you.
You're literally the best,
No matter what anyone else ever tries to tell you.

What Does It Take to Be Yourself?

What does it require
To move the ways you wish to move?
What do you have to feel like
To be congruent with your dream life?

Are you a square peg trying to fit into a round hole?
Are you well-rounded enough to roll into your preferred
life?
Are you in alignment with the vibration of your highest
self?
Are you on track for your greatness on your path to
success?

If not, why aren't you?
Is it that you're afraid of all the power that you hold?
So you're trying to suppress yourself by continuing to play
small?

Do you know who you are?

You are tremendous and infinitely powerful.
You're a divine being pretending to be a mere mortal.

It's okay to be afraid of your power at first.
And as you get to know and understand yourself more,
It's okay to relax into the fullness of who you are
At your own, perfect pace in divine right timing.

If you'd rather not see what you're capable of right now,
It's okay to stay who you are right where you are.

But if you'd like to become more of who you could be,
That's okay, too.
There's no better or worse decision.
Superiority is only an illusion.
And there's never any hurry.
You have your whole lifetime to figure yourself out.
Don't worry about any of the supposed competition.

It's all just hypothetical versions of you
That come into existence
By living out the choices
That you either make or let yourself go along with.

And whichever you
That you choose to be
Is always okay and entirely up to you
Just make sure that you're confident in your decisions.
To grow in any direction or to remain the same.

And if you'd like something to move any differently,
You must make the necessary adjustments
To allow room for more freedom and mobility.

You must prioritize yourself
And do what it takes to be your preferred self.
Are you acting as if even the thing you're concerned about
Is already resolved in the future?

Do you really trust the life that you live?
Do you really believe that all things are working on your
behalf?
And transpiring in alignment with your highest good?

Do you believe in yourself to make it through?
Do you know that you're more than capable?
Do you realize that it's already over and you did it?

You already won.
All there is to do now is act like it.
Do what you already did
Retrace your steps.
Find the clues that you left for you.

Look inside.
Follow the path that you set for yourself.
You've already paved the way.
Only you know what it is.
Only you can guide yourself.

All I, or even anyone, can do
Is affirm you and support you,
Because it's already done.
There's nothing more we can do.

Ignorance is Power

Knowledge creates parameters
For information to operate within.
But we can only work with what we know,
As everything outside of that is incompatible,
And therefore wouldn't make any sense.

If you know one thing to be true,
Then its opposite must be false.
If you assume one thing to be true,
Then you are also assuming another to be false

In both instances, the other may or may not be true,
But logic wouldn't give it a chance to even be considered.
This can be used to your benefit or detriment.

If you're attempting to do a thing,
And you know for a fact that you'll succeed,
Then you won't entertain any doubt or uncertainty,
And will then be more magnetic toward your desired
outcome.

If you assume that you will succeed,
Without full consideration of all the variables,
You might confidently meet
What we commonly refer to as failures.

If you think you know something about a person,
You won't even ask them.
You'll just assume it's true and move accordingly.
This limits the person in question
To a box of your own limitations.
They could be so much more

Or much less than you assume to know,
And even if they prove it either way,
You'll just dismiss it as a fluke.

The universe operates in this exact same way.
Everything you think you know
Becomes a self-fulfilling prophecy.
Everything that you neglect to decide
Is fueling the fire of uncertainty
That could burn down the bridges
To your desired reality.

If you acknowledge that there's a bit of uncertainty in any
situation,
Then you leave room to be pleasantly or unpleasantly
surprised.
Use this strategically
Limited awareness has advantages.

Decide to pay no mind and give no attention
To anything that contradicts any of your intentions.
Focus your awareness on the only reality
In which everything works out
The way that you envision

Doubt your doubts.
Turn that negative into a positive.
Trust yourself.
Believe that you are capable
And that all of your desires are inevitable.

Be limited by your knowingness.
And choose your assumptions wisely
For these are precisely how you define your life.

Know that all of your problems are in the gym,
Working themselves out on their own.
You might as well go join them.

Your dreams are chasing you equally.
They're looking at you,
Admiring you from afar,
Waiting for you to discover who you are
And release everything that's holding you back from them.

What you want wants you more.
Why do you think you care so much?
Everything you desire is a part of who you are.
Your dream life dreams about having you in it.
It's out there waiting for you to experience it.
Waiting for you to eventually embody it.
And allow yourself to relax into it.

Know that you are supported by the entirety of existence.
And leave no room for uncertainty.
Reduce the options for what you will accept
And allow yourself to receive from the universe.

Limit them to an inevitable resolution
With all the room to surprise you with the how.
Be unwaveringly confident that the thing you're stressing
about
Is actually benefiting you,
Even if you have no idea how or why.

You're not meant to know everything right away.
That part is really none of your business.
All you have to do is limit your awareness
And focus on your manifestations.
Be grateful for the fact that they're on their way.

What Do You Feel?

Things can appear spontaneously
And seem like they came out of the blue,
But have been in the works since the dawn of eternity.

Synchronicity is the fact that before you existed,
Everything you could ever want, need, or prefer
Was set into motion at the dawn of eternity.

Every outcome in every reality already exists
And has been set to exist since the beginning of existence.
Every end, every destination, every goal
has all been set in stone
from the very beginning.
And there's nothing you can do about it.

Every inevitability and every impossibility.
They're all already happening,
And will unfold eventually.

Every future has been fulfilled in the end from the start.
Everything has already ceased to exist when it's all said and
done.
The death of you, the universe,
And everything you could ever know and love
Has already occurred every possible way.
Good, bad, happy, sad, orange, yellow, gray
They all happened in the best and worst of ways.

You get to decide which way to go now,
To figure out which ending you'd like to see.
But the whole time,
It's really about who you intend to be.

So how do you feel?
Do you feel like you're on track?
If not, find a way to navigate yourself
You do this by feeling your way around.
Emotions are how we make sense of what goes down,
So pay attention to everything that comes up.

Be grateful and embody all of your emotions.
Everything you perceive and interpret is important.
You feel your way through life
Like traversing a hallway in the dark.
You have to work with whatever you perceive to guide you
This is the journey of embodying your emotions.

If you feel a feeling you deem negative,
Go ahead and feel it anyway.
It'll go away faster when you let it in and let it out.
Let your feelings flow through you
Or they'll get trapped deep inside you.
Your issues could end up in your tissues

Honestly, a lot of us are emotionally constipated.
We have so many feelings and emotions to dump
That have been with us since childhood.
Some of us, even from the womb or pre-conception.

And we're torn up in the root
Because we haven't found a way
To let our pent-up emotions out
To see the light of day.

I promise you'll feel better
when you finally let it out.
Drink some water, it'll help
Do things to make yourself feel cared about.

Whatever you need to do to feel better, go do it.
Play some music and dance or sing,
Or do anything invigorating.
Whatever you can do to get in the zone and have fun!

But don't do someone else's version of fun
If it's not true and authentic to you.
Don't sing a song you don't like to impress anyone
Especially anyone that you like even less.

Play your own drum.
So you can dance to your own rhythm.
Bake your own cake
So you can have it and eat it, too.
Make up your own song
So you can sing it however you choose to.

Every feeling is a choice,
But we make them as a collective.
You didn't fall out of a coconut tree.
You exist within the context
Of all that came before you.
Sometimes, if you want to find freedom,
You have to undo what's already been done.

It's easier than it looks
It's all about altering your perception.
Although it seems rigid,
Reality is malleable
If you take matters into your own hands,
You can bend them with your will.
Because there is no spoon.
It's all a simulation.

Take action to release your restrictions.
Release the mental prisons you've locked yourself in.
Find a way out of the shackles you've been stuck in.
And find a way to feel like yourself once again.

What Can We Do?

The matrix is a game,
And there's only one player.
It's you and you're playing yourself.

Both sides are of the same coin.
But they're built to oppose each other.
The systems were intentionally designed that way.
And we've allowed them to be,
So they continue to stay.

Nothing will happen if we don't do what it takes.
If we don't stick together,
Everything will continue to fall apart.

It's already toppling over.
These systems are falling down.
And when they crumble,
What will we do with the rubble?
Where will we go from where we end up?

Will we be able to clean up the messes we've made?
Will we be able to work together as a species on this planet
And come together to make it all better?

Can we even get along with ourselves?
Do you even agree with yourself?

If your mind says one thing,
And your body another,
Who's really in charge,
And who truly runs the show?

What about your spirit?
Do you listen to your heart?
All it tells you to do is love.

Do you truly love thy neighbor?
Do you truthfully love yourself?
In all the ways you know how to?

Do you respect your own boundaries?
Do you know your own limits?
Do you respect everyone else the same way?

Imagine if we all did just that

What would it look like if we could see eye to eye?
What would it feel like if we harnessed all our energy
And used it creatively and productively?

What could we accomplish if we operated in unison
And strived for harmony with nature as all of humanity?

Where would we be as a people
If we respected everyone else's opinions and values?
And maybe even other's religions?

What if we all celebrated our differences
And used them to complement our weaknesses?
What if we filled all our voids with love
And stopped pretending we don't all feel the same way?

Imagine if we worked together as a people
To achieve goals that meant something useful.

What if we all felt all of our emotions
Truly, fully, and deeply,

And then found productive and creative ways to express
them?

What if we all acted like we knew what we were made of?
What if held ourselves to standards of divinity?
What if we were radically honest?

What if we acted as one people on one planet?
What if we chose to shed light on darkness and cover it
with love?
What if we stood in our power
And stopped trying to take it away from others?

Where would we go?
What would we do?
Think about it.
We'd be unstoppable as a species.

But right now,
We need to be stopped.

Just long enough for us to pause to catch our breath
Because it seems that we've entirely lost it.
And we don't even know where to look
All the answers are in the last place anyone wants to look,
Within.

If we all just took some time to pause, relax, and breathe,
Then everything would be okay.
It'll be okay either way,
It's just easier to be at peace until we get there.

We all want to be right but we hope we're already right.
We all want to be comfortable right where we are.
We all want results, but who's willing to do the work?
Who even knows what work should be done?

The only work is to love,
So start with yourself.

Love Somebody

Are you happy with yourself?
More importantly,
Is your self happy with you?

Is your body happy to hold you?
Are you grateful to it?
Does your body feel like you care for it
Or are you just using it?

Is your body just a means to an end for you?
Is your body truly somebody that you love?
We're always looking for somebody to give to,
But do you even give to your own body?

Do you feed it what it craves or what you think you want to
eat?
Do you trust your gut or use your intuitive instincts?
Do you listen to yourself?
Do you care about how you feel?
Do you push your body beyond its limits
Even when it told you it was through?

Are you really just using you?
That's what it seems like sometimes.
And you expect someone to come along and care for you?
How could you?

I'm for real, how could you actually?
How could you honestly care about yourself better?
How can you show yourself that you love your body more?
How can you let yourself know
That you truly appreciate everything you are?
Is there anything you can do just for you?

We work so hard all the time to give and give and give to
others.
Some of us more than others, but that's not the point.
What I'm meaning to say
Is at the end of the day,
If you really want to love somebody,
Then start with your own.

Water the flowers in your garden first
Let the rain come and take care of everyone else's
Mind the business that pays you
Don't get caught up dealing with the monkeys
In somebody else's circus

I was once told
That a great leader puts himself first
And then himself second,
And then himself once again for third.
And then everyone else is tied for what's left,
But there would be so much more for them
If you gave yourself everything you needed from you first.

If I give you my last dollar,
Knowing I could've done more with it,
I robbed myself in the future
By emptying my cup in the present.

No one can pour from an empty cup.
You can't feed anyone from an empty plate.
Take care of yourself first,
And second and third.
That's mind, body, spirit,
Or past, present, and future.

Do everything you told yourself you would eventually do.
Stop procrastinating your priorities,
Stop neglecting your needs,
And stop canceling any of your commitments to yourself.

Your body needs you
Just as much as you need it.
It's a group effort,
A win-win situation.

Although sometimes it seems
Like there are a couple conflicting needs,
It's all just a matter of communication.
Your system is nervous to speak to you.
Maybe it's because it likes you.

Everything it does is to keep you alive.
Self-preservation is the first law of nature.
Maybe your anxiety is an abundance of energy
That your body manifested because it thought it saw a
threat.

If your heart is racing,
Give it a reason to beat harder,
And for your lungs to have to breathe deeper.
Exhaust yourself.

You can only relieve the stress by releasing it.
Sometimes you have to tense up to calm down.
Speed up to slow down.
Or else you'll stay energetically stuck up.

You have to push yourself in order to relax.
It's the way the body was designed.
It was built to keep you alive.

Work with it and use it to your advantage.
Make friends with it and do what it says.
Move how it feels.
And think with it, not for it.
It knows more than you do.

All your cells are sentient.
Your organs are alive.
They communicate with each other,
and even you if you listen.

Connect to your intuition.
All the answers are within you,
Although solutions first manifest
As problems to be resolved.

What About Her?

How do you think the Earth feels?
How often do you think She feels considered?
She provides so much for us
And we barely even say thank you.

Who raised us?
Did we forget we have two parents?
Even though one of them is more or less invisible?
We pray to the one we don't see,
And forget about the one that's always there?

How does that work?
I think we should take some time
To appreciate the Earth
And remind Her of Her worth.

We sing praises to the Most High,
And praise our Heavenly Father,
But we rarely acknowledge the ground beneath our feet as
our Earthly Mother.

We are the children of two parents,
And they both deserve recognition.
How would you feel if you were Her?

As a little thought experiment,
Put yourself in Her shoes,
And let's reflect on how we've been treating Her,
Collectively as humans.

We've been leaving Her out of so many things,
Forgetting that She has Her own feelings.
We personify the Sun,

Then disrespect and neglect the Earth,
Down to demonizing the feminine
In most of our mythologies.
Don't even get me started on the patriarchy…

Why have we forgotten who provided our every meal?

Yes, the Sun helped it grow,
But it grew from the Earth.
Yes, the Sun gives life,
But so does Mother Earth
Yes, He does wonderful things,
But so does She
Why do we forget about Her?

She hears your cries.
Do you listen to Her?
She sees your tears.
Do you care about Hers?

Do you let Her know that you're grateful
For all that She's given you?
Or anything She's done for you?
Do you love the Earth nearly as much as She loves you?

It makes sense that in order to use and be trusted
With the goodness, magic, and love of the Earth,
That we'd be trusted to do good things with them.
And at the very least, not just take them and make things
worse.

Otherwise, She might as well
Flood Herself, wash Herself, and cleanse Herself to rid
Herself
Of the pesky little people that never
Respect Her, value Her, appreciate Her, or treasure Her.

Unconditional love without boundaries is self-harm
We put Her through hell and she loves us still.
Maybe we can learn a thing or two from Her.
Maybe She has a little bit of wisdom inside Her.

I'm sure She's been around long enough to understand
Quite a bit about space and energetic boundaries.
I'm sure She can tell who does and doesn't care about Her
authentically.

A woman's intuition is a powerful thing.
I'm sure Mother Earth's discernment can feel the wills
Of the characters that are cast upon her surface
In this, and every, stage of Life.

What are we doing here, dwelling on Her surface?
What are we making of these lives we've been given?
Why do we deserve to be alive?

Are we going to appreciate what's been invested in us?
Or will we depreciate until we plummet back down into
Her,
Empty-handed after taking so much our whole lives?

Will Earth be receiving you gracefully,
Or will She have shaken you off like a flea?
I'm sure you've killed a bug before,
Or gotten rid of something you didn't particularly care for.

Don't be scared now, She doesn't think like us
It's a good thing Mother Earth is gracious to us.
All She wants for us to do is be grateful and reciprocate,
So let's give Her the same love that She's given to us.

I'm so glad that She loves us as Her children.
I'm grateful that we've been given space to grow and time
to learn.
I'm so joyful to have been given life.
And I think She'd be grateful if more of us were as well.

I know that was pretty intense, dark, and even a bit
macabre,
But we're all gonna die regardless.
I was raised to leave things better than I found them,
So pardon my harshness,
I'm simply passionate about this.

My goal in even writing this
Is to stir up the people and shake up the earth,
Ultimately, to spin us in a new direction.
I'm here to start a revolution on this planet
To put us on a new path.
A higher trajectory, if you will.

We can make the world a better place,
And love both parents appropriately.
But only if you choose it.
And only if you'd allow it.

You decide what you do with your life.
You choose what you make of what you have.
You create your reality with your free will.
You write the script and direct it as you act it.

You have to get things to their breaking point,
And cross the threshold for them to change states
In order to exist within a new range of frequencies.
We decide what our tipping points are.
We decide how much we want to go through
Before we change our patterns and alter our cycles.

So lighten up and have fun as you play your role,
Because that's precisely how we roll on this planet
Upgrade your circle and improve your orbit.
Give light to the people you've attracted to your circuit.

Be a force for good.
Love thyself and love thy neighbor,
And always remember
To say thank you to your Mother.

Surrender

Existing is a lot.

It can be very challenging, lonely, arduous, draining,
Intense, dark, and deeply depressing
In all sorts of negative feelings and experiences.

It can also be filled with love, joy, peace, bliss,
Laughter, perfection, enlightenment, abundance,
And truly all things good.

In fact, life was designed to be joyful and full of love.
Life on earth, however, was also designed to be full
Of polarity, duality, and contrast.
The high highs would be meaningless without the low
lows.

How boring would your favorite song be
If all the pitches were the same,
And all the melodies were instead monotonous?
How lame would life be if every day was the same?

It's a blessing that the roller coaster of life has its twists and
turns
Mixed in with the exhilarating ups and downs
That sometimes make you want to scream.

Life can often feel chaotic and even uncontrollable,
But what if I told you that you were the one
That designed the roller coaster of your life?

What would you think of the twists and turns
If you knew that you put them there?
How would you feel if you knew

That your feelings themselves direct the ride?
What would you think if you knew that your thoughts were
the ride itself?

How would you act if you knew that you truly
Had free and complete control of the roller coaster of your
life
Through your thoughts and words manifesting through
your actions?

As humans, it's difficult to conceive the notion
that we are actually in charge of, sometimes, anything in
our lives.
We sometimes even feel like we can't even control
The thoughts within our own minds.
I'm here to tell you that we have complete control
Over everything in our lives at the highest and lowest
levels.

How?

By surrendering it.

You gain control when you surrender control.
You win the fight when you stop fighting.
You see when you stop looking so hard
And instead, let whatever it is find you.
You know things when you stop thinking long enough
For real insights to make themselves known to you.

Nothing ever happens through sheer force.
Nothing harmonious or productive at least.
Everything happens when it is meant to,
When it is chosen,
And when the divine right conditions allow for them to
occur.

Trying harder doesn't get you through traffic any faster
Than waiting for the cars ahead of you
To simply move when they move.

Life flows at the divine right pace.

Stressing, being anxious,
Wanting things to happen before they're meant to
(That might not even be meant to be at all),
And otherwise rushing yourself,
God or anything else in existence
Is fruitless, to say the least.

Relax, allow, and surrender to life.
Surrender to the fact that everything will be okay
And consider that everything has always been okay.
Allow things to occur when they're meant to.
Allow the roller coaster to be fun, pleasant, and enjoyable.

Trust that you are a divine co-creator of your life
experience.
Trust that all of your problems are in the gym,
Working themselves out.

Know that you are connected, inextricably,
To the source of all creation.
That you are one with the divine,
One with the all,
And you are that I AM.

We are all the great I AM,
Collectively,
Together, WE ARE

We comprise that which is.
We are made of the one divine substance,
Which is God itself,
Made manifest as all that exists.

All.
Including you.

Be not afraid of your divinity,
Embrace your divine spark,
Live as if you were made in the image and likeness of your
creator
And create that which you wish to experience.
Create that which you wish to see in the world

Sit on your throne.
Take your rightful place in the kingdom and queendom of
heaven,
And create heaven on this earth.

With great power comes great responsibility.
This means that we have the greatest responsibility
For we have the greatest power in existence.

We are God.

We channel the power of life itself for all that we do,
From breathing to alchemizing, to doing number two.

The love of God is the magic that makes all of life happen.
Love is the only moving force in the universe.

Surrender to love, surrender to life, and surrender to God.
And surrender to the fact
that you are love, you are life, you are God.
And that these three things are one and the same.

At the End of the Day, We're All Human

I'm just a person,
Just like everybody else.
We're all regular humans.
Nothing all that special about any one in particular.

We're all God's favorite,
But we're all unique.
We exist in vastly different ways,
All of which are equally fascinating and compelling.

And with compulsion comes repulsion.
With love comes hate.
We exist in polarity,
Which just feeds the confusion.
We can't come together if we're going in opposite
directions.

We've been living life at the extremes
With some of us being stuck anywhere in between.
Some of them could be lost,
Maybe some of them content.
But who's happy?
Only the ones that have chosen to be.

I'm here to implore you to choose for yourself.
While still learning and relearning what it means even to be
myself.
I'm rediscovering who I am by finding myself
And I've found that I see myself everywhere I look.

Ultimately, I realized I was only searching for myself
And that all I had to do was relax and be myself
Now I encourage you to be yourself
By sharing a bit about what I've learned about myself.

I hid a whole personality in an alternate mentality,
Pretending not to be who I was.
I depressed myself by repressing myself,
I didn't let myself breathe or be free.
I was learning what it means to be me.

I had to learn that it was safe to be who I was
I had to learn to love myself by watching myself
Pour out the love I needed for my growth onto others.
I had to watch myself get neglected while I cared for so
many others

I looked past the sadness in my eyes
From watching my own self die
A slow and painful death.
I endorsed my own demise.

Sometimes the way to learn to live is by dying.
That's why the old me had to die
For the real me to start living.
The inner me made me kill myself.
So good morning.
It's good to be alive.

I've decided that who I am, as I am is good enough,
And that how I am, where I am is actually fine.
I don't have to have it all figured out.
I've done enough, and I'll continue to improve over time.

I'm truly just getting started.
This is only the beginning.

It's the Prelude to Suite 1,
And I've only just begun
Now that I exist,
It's time for me to have some fun.

It's a one-man show,
And a marvelous play.
It's a privilege to see myself every day.
I'm a badge of honor and I'm something to be proud of.
Though I'm a failure to some,
I'm a success to others.
Who's actually right?
The world may never know.

But I know who I am, and that's nothing.
I'm a figment of your imagination.
I'm just a picture in your mind's eye.
You can paint me how you see me,
But that only shows me the things that you see in yourself.
No matter how much beauty or darkness you may see,
I have nothing to do with what anyone thinks of me.

I give myself permission to exist.
I allow myself to take up my own space.
I release the pressure to be more than I am.
I release the tension of playing smaller than I am.

I simply am myself,
And there's nothing else to do,
But embrace who I am with love as I bloom.

And if you are yourself,
And your goal is to be yourself,
Then there's nothing more you could possibly do.

So keep up the good work,
And love what you do.
No matter who you are,
I will always choose to love you.
<3